COOL CRAFTS FOR KIDS

PIPE CLEANER PROJECTS

Jane Yates

WINDMILL
BOOKS ™

Published in 2017 by **Windmill Books**, an Imprint of Rosen Publishing
29 East 21st Street, New York, NY 10010

Developed and produced for Rosen by BlueAppleWorks Inc.

Creative Director: Melissa McClellan
Managing Editor for BlueAppleWorks: Melissa McClellan
Designer: T.J. Choleva
Photo Research: Jane Reid
Editor: Kelly Spence
Craft Artisans: Jane Yates (p. 8, 10, 12, 14, 16, 20, 22, 24, 26, 28)

Photo Credits: cover left sashahaltam/Shutterstock; cover right pathdoc/Shutterstock; title page
background, TOC, page tops Dana Zurki/Shutterstock; cover, back cover, title page, p. 4, 6 – 31
Austen Photography; p. 5 left to right and top to bottom: Eric Boucher/Shutterstock; Samantha
Roberts/Shutterstock; valzan/Shutterstock; Stock Up/Shutterstock; Crackerclips/Dreamstime.com;
antpkr/Thinkstock

Cataloging-in-Publication Data

Names: Yates, Jane.
Title: Pipe cleaner projects / Jane Yates.
Description: New York : Windmill Books, 2017. | Series: Cool crafts for kids | Includes index.
Identifiers: ISBN 9781499482379 (pbk.) | ISBN 9781499482386 (library bound) |
  ISBN 9781508192831 (6 pack)
Subjects: LCSH: Pipe cleaner craft--Juvenile literature.
Classification: LCC TT880.Y38 2017 | DDC 745.5--dc23

Manufactured in the United States of America
CPSIA Compliance Information: Batch #BW17PK:
For Further Information contact Rosen Publishing, New York, New York at 1-800-237-9932

CONTENTS

GETTING STARTED

You don't need a lot of materials for pipe cleaner projects! These flexible, fuzzy wires are also called **chenille** stems. They come in all sorts of shapes, sizes, and colors. Some even sparkle!

You can purchase everything you need at a craft store or dollar store. Organize your supplies in boxes or plastic bins. That way, they are ready for when you want to create pipe cleaner projects!

SPARKLY PIPE CLEANERS

BUMPY PIPE CLEANERS

REGULAR PIPE CLEANERS

FAT PIPE CLEANERS

GIANT PIPE CLEANERS

FAT MARKER

Did You Know?

Pipe cleaners were invented in the late 1800s to clean smoking pipes. Today they are mostly used for fun crafts.

PENCIL

SCISSORS

CARD STOCK

GLUE

TAPE

A note about measurements

Measurements are given in US format with metric in parentheses. The metric conversion is rounded to make it easier to measure.

TECHNIQUES

Have fun while making your pipe cleaner projects! Your projects do not have to look just like the ones in this book. You can use whatever colors you like. Be creative and use your imagination!

Use the following techniques to create your pipe cleaner crafts.

SPIRAL

● Hold one end of a pipe cleaner against a pencil. Tightly wind the pipe cleaner around the pencil, then slip it off.

LARGE SPIRAL

● Hold one end of a pipe cleaner against a fat marker. Coil the pipe cleaner around the marker, then slide it off.

BALL

● Wrap a pipe cleaner around the end of a pencil a few times, then wrap around it again, slip off the pencil, and wrap it until you have a ball shape. For a bigger ball shape, use fat or jumbo pipe cleaners.

CUTTING A PIPE CLEANER

● Use scissors to trim pipe cleaners. Be very careful when cutting pipe cleaners. The wires are sharp!

CONNECT

- Twist the ends of two pipe cleaners together to connect them. Make sure the sharp ends are not sticking up.

TWIST

- Lay two pipe cleaners side by side. Starting at one end, twist them together.

FLAT SPIRAL

- Fold the tip of a pipe cleaner. Then wind the rest of the pipe cleaner in a tight circle around it. Place the pipe cleaner on a table to keep it flat.

SECURE

- Hook the tip of one pipe cleaner around another to join them.

Tip

For safety, bend back any sharp points at the ends of the pipe cleaners or put a dab of glue on sharp ends of anything you will be wearing.

BE PREPARED

- Read through the instructions and make sure you have all the materials you need.
- Clean up when you are finished with a project. Put away your materials so they are ready for next time.

BE SAFE

- Ask for help when you need it.
- Ask for permission to borrow tools.
- Be careful when using scissors.

GROOVY GLASSES

You'll Need:

✔ One green pipe cleaner
✔ Two yellow pipe cleaners
✔ Two orange pipe cleaners

1 Curl the end of a pipe cleaner into a circle. Attach the end to the rest of the pipe cleaner as shown.

2 Form the other end into a circle and join it to the pipe cleaner. Leave about ½ inch (1 cm) of straight pipe cleaner in between the two circles.

3 For each arm, twist an orange and a yellow pipe cleaner together.

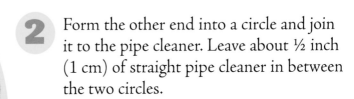

4 Wrap each arm around the outer edge of the circles.

5 Curve the ends so they hook over your ears. Try the glasses on to make sure they fit. Cut off any extra pipe cleaner.

Curl the end back onto itself.

6 Fold the tips in so there are no sharp points at the ends.

FUNKY FLOWERS

You'll Need:

✔ One bumpy pink pipe cleaner
✔ Two fat orange pipe cleaners
✔ Two yellow pipe cleaners
✔ Two green pipe cleaners
✔ Glue

1 For **petals**, cut a bumpy pink pipe cleaner into three pieces as shown.

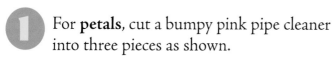

Wrap around centers

2 Bundle the three pieces together. Wrap a yellow pipe cleaner around the thinner center sections. Leave some extra yellow pipe cleaner sticking out each side.

3 Fan the petals into a half-circle shape.

Make loops

Twist yellow stem

4 Use a green pipe cleaner as a stem. Make two loops for leaves. Then, twist the ends of the yellow pipe cleaner around the top of the stem to attach the flower.

DAISY

1 For petals, use a fat orange pipe cleaner and make three loops. Leave a small length at one end and a longer length at the other as shown.

2 Pull the three loops together and wrap the shorter end around the center.

3 Repeat Steps 1 and 2 to make three more petals. Use the longer ends to join the two halves together.

4 Wind a flat yellow spiral and tuck the end underneath. Glue the spiral to the center of the flower. Attach a stem if desired.

Tip

Use a pipe cleaner to wrap several flowers together to make a beautiful bouquet!

JAZZY JEWELRY

You'll Need:

✔ Assorted pipe cleaners
✔ Beads
✔ Tape

BRAIDED BRACELET

1 Twist together three pipe cleaners 1 inch (2.5 cm) from the ends. Tape the bundle to a desk or table. Start braiding the three pipe cleaners together.

Blue under white to center

White under pink to center

Pink under blue to center

2 Braid the entire bundle, then bend it into a circle. Twist the ends to close the loop.

Twist together

TWISTED BRACELET

Twist two pipe cleaners together. After 1 inch (2.5 cm) is twisted, slide a bead onto both pipe cleaners. Pinch at the bead and twist another 1 inch (2.5 cm) section. Add another bead. Repeat until you reach the end. Form the pipe cleaners into a circle and twist the ends together.

Add beads

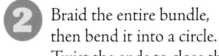

RING

For a braided ring, start with three shorter pieces of pipe cleaner. Braid the pieces together. After 1 inch (2.5 cm), add a bead to the center piece. Continue braiding until the ring fits your finger. Connect the ends and cut off any extra pieces.

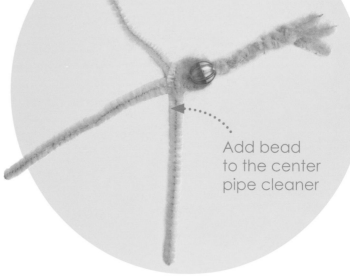

Add bead to the center pipe cleaner

NECKLACE

For a necklace, join two pipe cleaners together and then follow the bracelet instructions.

Tip

Glam it up! Try making jewelry with sparkly pipe cleaners!

COLORFUL COASTERS

You'll Need:

✔ Five blue pipe cleaners
✔ Five green pipe cleaners
✔ Ruler
✔ Scissors

1 Start with five blue pipe cleaners. Use scissors to trim 2½ inches (6 cm) off each pipe cleaner. Use a ruler to measure.

Wrap around and trim excess

2 Bundle the pipe cleaners together. Bend and wrap half of one pipe cleaner around the middle of the bundle. Wind it tightly around the bundle three times. Trim the extra off.

3 Arrange the ends like the **spokes** of a wheel.

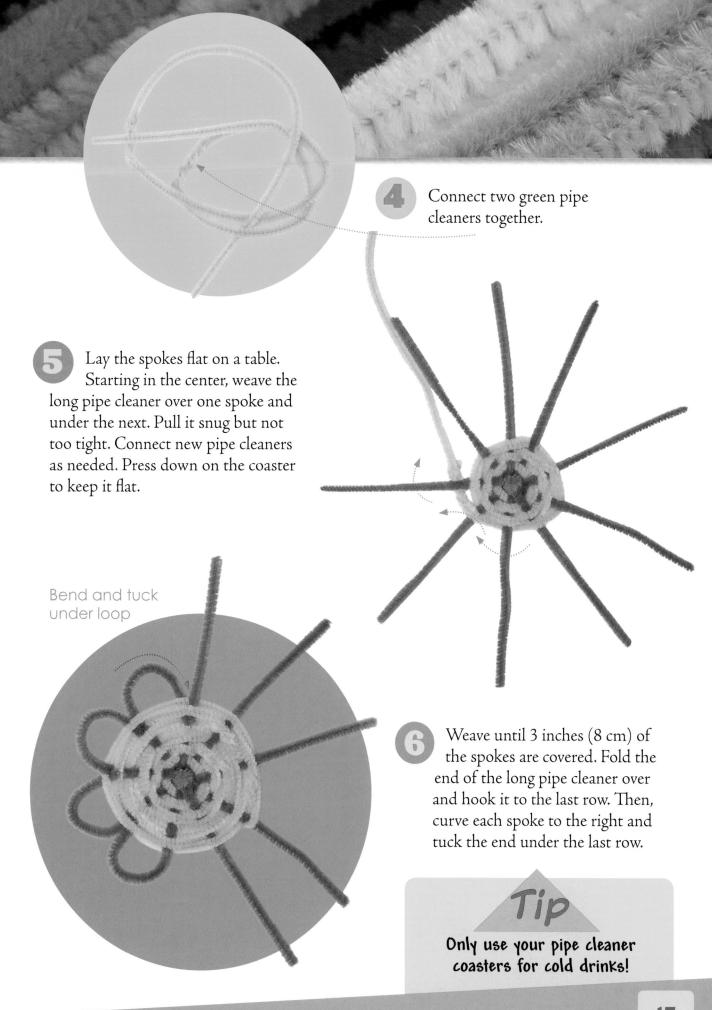

4 Connect two green pipe cleaners together.

5 Lay the spokes flat on a table. Starting in the center, weave the long pipe cleaner over one spoke and under the next. Pull it snug but not too tight. Connect new pipe cleaners as needed. Press down on the coaster to keep it flat.

Bend and tuck under loop

6 Weave until 3 inches (8 cm) of the spokes are covered. Fold the end of the long pipe cleaner over and hook it to the last row. Then, curve each spoke to the right and tuck the end under the last row.

Tip

Only use your pipe cleaner coasters for cold drinks!

FURRY FRIENDS

You'll Need:

✔ Two 18-inch (46 cm) giant tan pipe cleaners
✔ One giant brown pipe cleaner
✔ One giant orange pipe cleaner
✔ One brown pipe cleaner
✔ One striped pipe cleaner
✔ Glue
✔ Sequins or googly eyes
✔ A pencil and a fat marker

DOG

1 For the dog's body, coil the giant tan pipe cleaner around a fat marker. Leave about 1 inch (2.5 cm) of one end straight for the tail.

2 Cut a giant brown pipe cleaner in half. Coil each half around a pencil. For legs, bend each piece in half. Position the legs between the coils of the body.

Attach face and ears

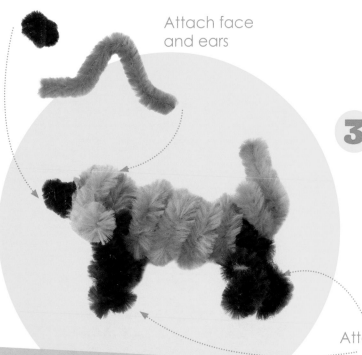

3 Make a ball with a brown pipe cleaner. Push it into the body coil. To make ears, cut a 4-inch (10 cm) piece of tan pipe cleaner. Fold it in half, curl the ends, and glue it to the head. Add sequins or googly eyes to the dog's face.

Attach legs

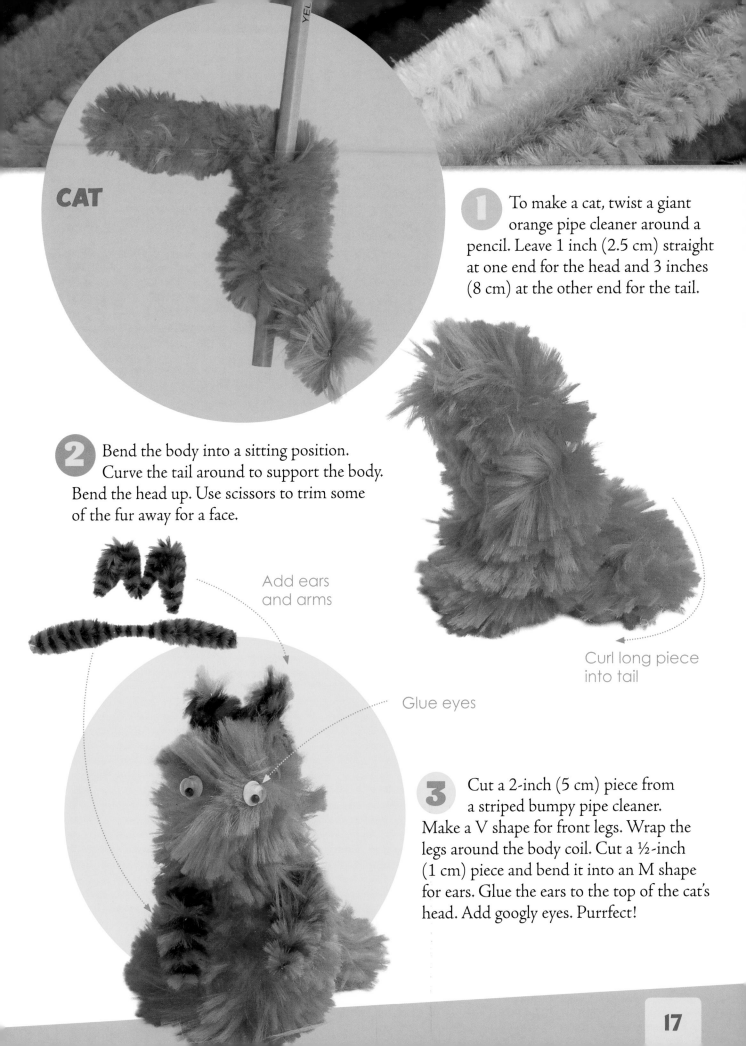

CAT

1 To make a cat, twist a giant orange pipe cleaner around a pencil. Leave 1 inch (2.5 cm) straight at one end for the head and 3 inches (8 cm) at the other end for the tail.

2 Bend the body into a sitting position. Curve the tail around to support the body. Bend the head up. Use scissors to trim some of the fur away for a face.

Add ears and arms

Curl long piece into tail

Glue eyes

3 Cut a 2-inch (5 cm) piece from a striped bumpy pipe cleaner. Make a V shape for front legs. Wrap the legs around the body coil. Cut a ½-inch (1 cm) piece and bend it into an M shape for ears. Glue the ears to the top of the cat's head. Add googly eyes. Purrfect!

RAINBOW VASE

You'll Need:

✔ Clean plastic bottle
✔ Double-sided tape
✔ Variety of pipe cleaners
✔ Scissors

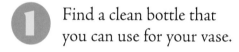

1 Find a clean bottle that you can use for your vase.

2 Choose the pipe cleaners you would like to use. The number will depend on how big the bottle is. Start with 20. Add more if needed.

3 Connect 10 pipe cleaners to form a single long pipe cleaner.

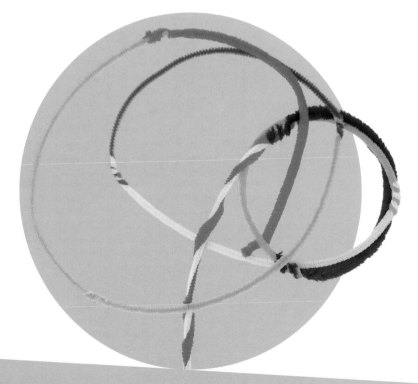

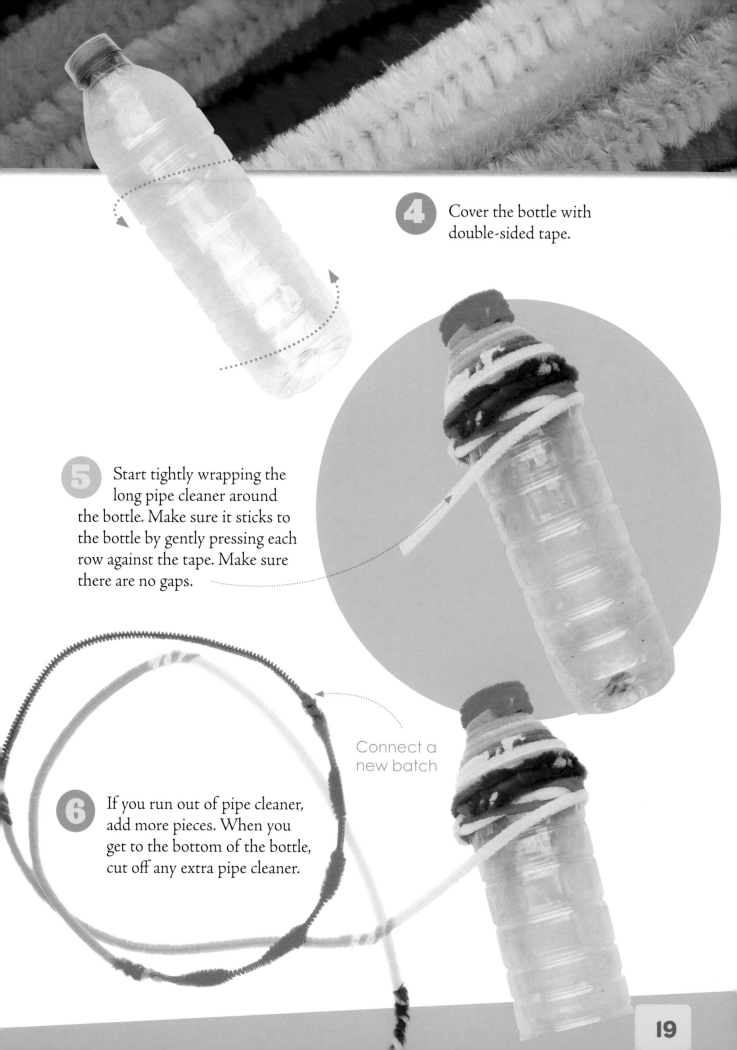

4 Cover the bottle with double-sided tape.

5 Start tightly wrapping the long pipe cleaner around the bottle. Make sure it sticks to the bottle by gently pressing each row against the tape. Make sure there are no gaps.

Connect a new batch

6 If you run out of pipe cleaner, add more pieces. When you get to the bottom of the bottle, cut off any extra pipe cleaner.

CROWN JEWELS

You'll Need:

✔ Sparkly silver pipe cleaners
✔ Sparkly gold pipe cleaners
✔ Plastic headband
✔ Self-stick jewels
✔ Scissors

TIARA

1 Join six silver pipe cleaners together. Wrap the pipe cleaner tightly around a headband. Bend the sharp ends in.

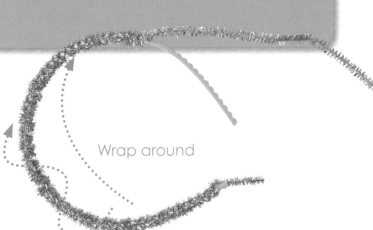

Wrap around

2 Bend one silver pipe cleaner into three points as shown. Center it on top of the headband. Twist the ends around the headband to attach it.

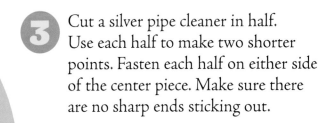

3 Cut a silver pipe cleaner in half. Use each half to make two shorter points. Fasten each half on either side of the center piece. Make sure there are no sharp ends sticking out.

4 Decorate your tiara with self-stick jewels.

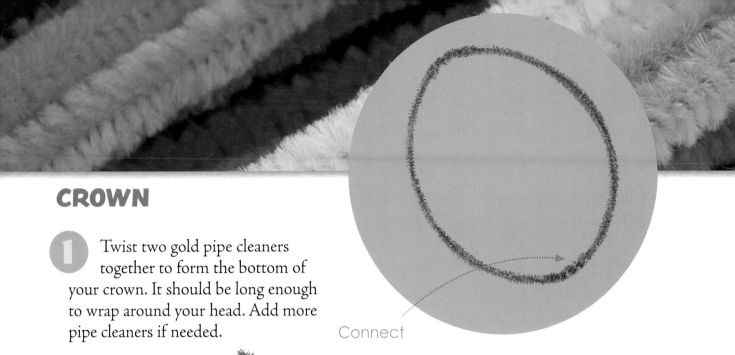

Connect

CROWN

1 Twist two gold pipe cleaners together to form the bottom of your crown. It should be long enough to wrap around your head. Add more pipe cleaners if needed.

2 For points, bend a gold pipe cleaner into an M shape. The ends should be slightly longer than the "V" in the middle.

3 Hook the M under the crown as shown. The "V" should sit against the base. Turn the ends of the M to face outward. Twist the ends to secure the M to the base. Make more M shapes and attach them around the whole circle.

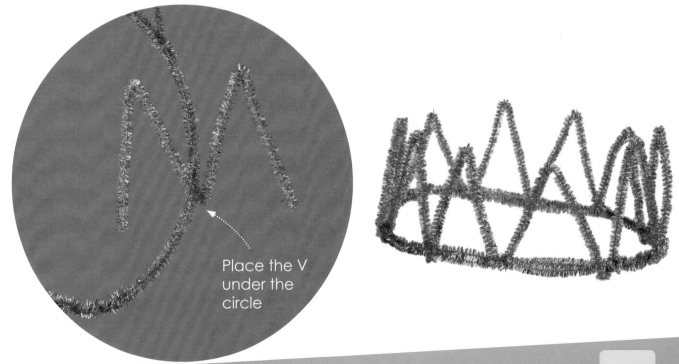

Place the V under the circle

MINI MONSTER

You'll Need:

✔ One fat green pipe cleaner
✔ Three purple pipe cleaners
✔ One sparkly gold pipe cleaner
✔ White card stock
✔ Googly eyes
✔ Glue
✔ Fat marker and a pencil
✔ Scissors

1 Roll a piece of card stock into a tube. Glue the ends together.

2 To make a spiral, wrap a fat green pipe cleaner around the marker. Glue one end of the tube to the inside of the spiral.

Glue the tube inside the ball

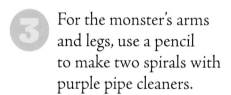

3 For the monster's arms and legs, use a pencil to make two spirals with purple pipe cleaners.

4 For the body, cut a purple pipe cleaner in half. Coil it around the marker.

Glue head to body

5 For legs, bend one spiral in half. Push it through the bottom of the body spiral. Use the second coil for arms. Glue the tube to the body spiral to attach the monster's head.

Join arms to body

Join legs to body

6 Cut the gold pipe cleaner into five equal pieces. Attach four pieces to the top of the head. Bend the tips. Bend the last piece in a zigzag and place it in the monster's hand.

Glue on teeth and eyes

7 Cut pointy teeth out of white card stock. Glue the teeth and googly eyes onto the monster's face.

NAME SIGN

You'll Need:

- ✔ Thin cardboard (a cereal box works well)
- ✔ Hole punch
- ✔ Five giant pipe cleaners
- ✔ A variety of pipe cleaners
- ✔ Double-sided tape
- ✔ Scissors
- ✔ Glue

1 Cut a rectangle out of thin cardboard using the measurements shown.

3¼ inches (8 cm) high

9 inches (23 cm) wide

Punch 2 holes

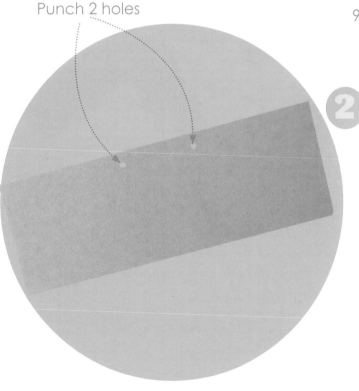

2 Use a hole punch to make two holes in the top center of the cardboard.

3 For the handle, thread the ends of a giant pipe cleaner through each hole. Twist them together at the back.

Twist

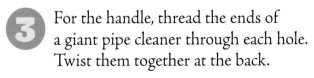

4 On the back of the sign, place a strip of double-sided tape on each end. Wrap four giant pipe cleaners around the cardboard, pressing the ends into the tape.

5 Form the letters of your name out of pipe cleaners.

6 Glue the letters to the sign.

Tip

Hang your name sign on the doorknob to your bedroom.

HEART ORNAMENT

You'll Need:
✔ Two fat pink pipe cleaners
✔ Three fat red pipe cleaners
✔ Scissors
✔ Glue
✔ Thread

1 Twist together one pink and one red pipe cleaner.

Twist

2 Connect the ends.
Bend the pipe cleaner into a heart shape.

3 Repeat Steps 1 and 2 so that you have two hearts.

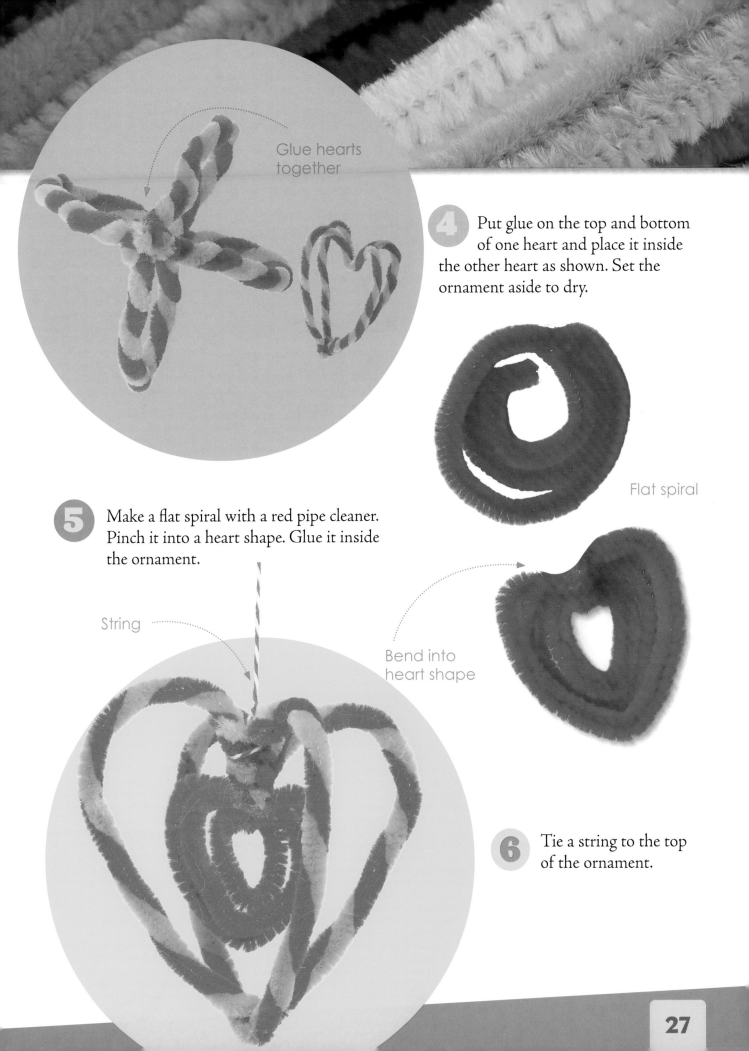

Glue hearts together

4 Put glue on the top and bottom of one heart and place it inside the other heart as shown. Set the ornament aside to dry.

Flat spiral

5 Make a flat spiral with a red pipe cleaner. Pinch it into a heart shape. Glue it inside the ornament.

String

Bend into heart shape

6 Tie a string to the top of the ornament.

PIPE CLEANER PEOPLE

You'll Need:

✔ Four blue pipe cleaners
✔ Several fuzzy pipe cleaners
✔ One fat purple pipe cleaner
✔ Scissors
✔ Glue

1 Join four pipe cleaners together. Fold it in half. Twist the pipe cleaner to form a small loop at the top.

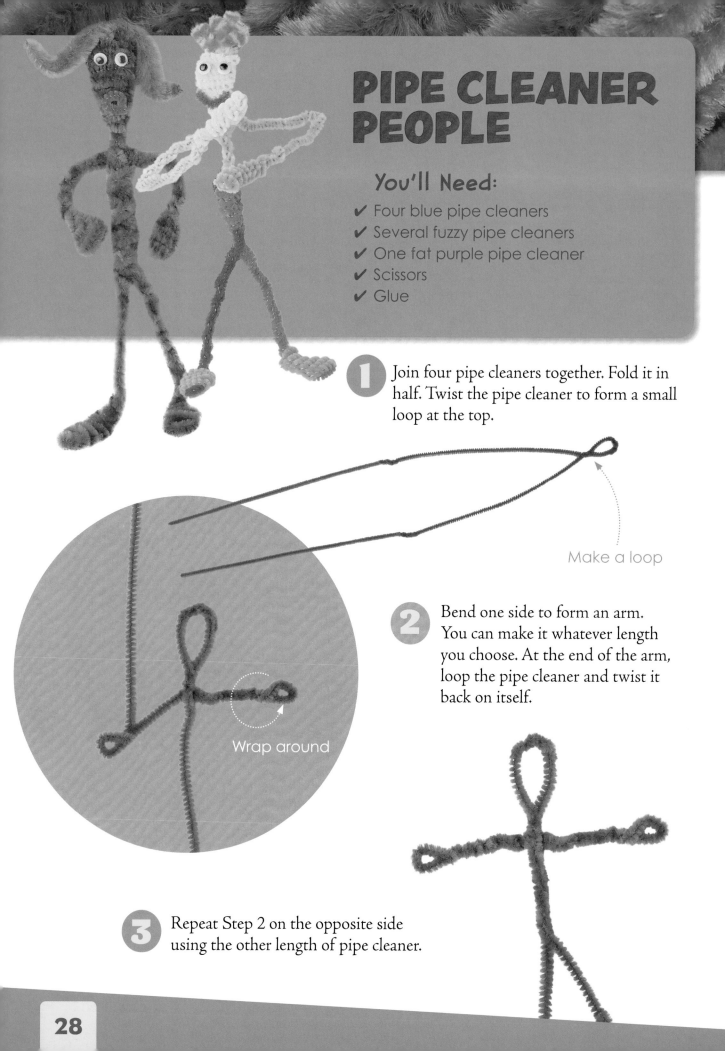

Make a loop

Wrap around

2 Bend one side to form an arm. You can make it whatever length you choose. At the end of the arm, loop the pipe cleaner and twist it back on itself.

3 Repeat Step 2 on the opposite side using the other length of pipe cleaner.

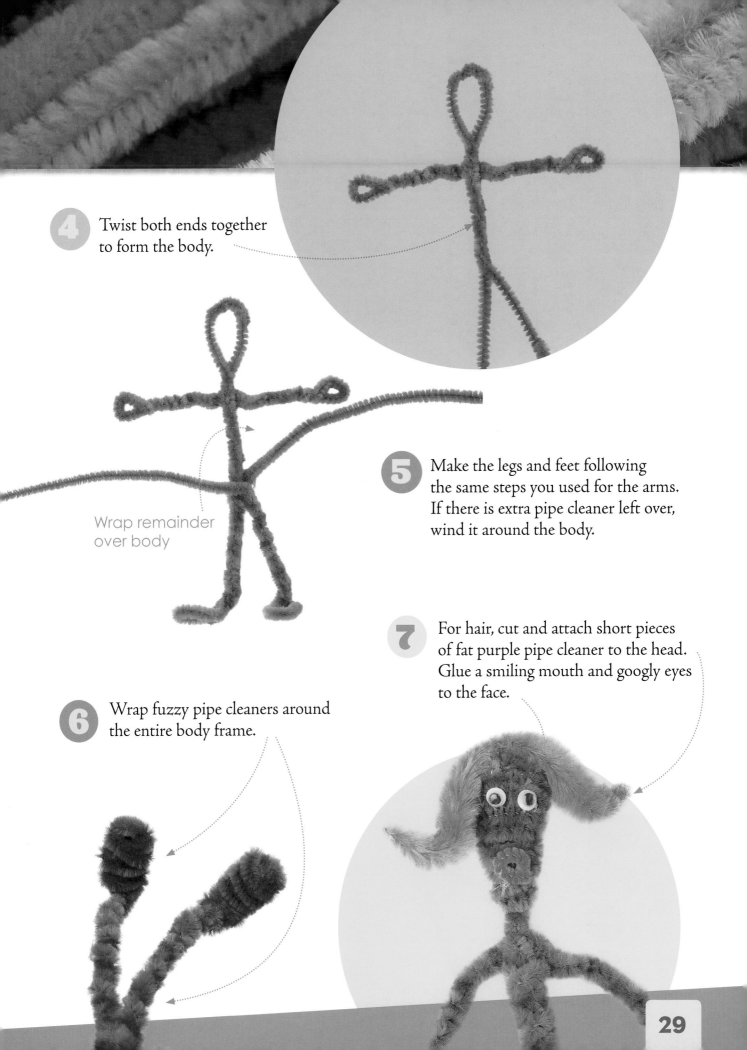

4 Twist both ends together to form the body.

Wrap remainder over body

5 Make the legs and feet following the same steps you used for the arms. If there is extra pipe cleaner left over, wind it around the body.

7 For hair, cut and attach short pieces of fat purple pipe cleaner to the head. Glue a smiling mouth and googly eyes to the face.

6 Wrap fuzzy pipe cleaners around the entire body frame.

FUZZY BUGS

You'll Need:

✔ One giant blue pipe cleaner
✔ One fat red pipe cleaner
✔ Two brown pipe cleaners
✔ Eight fat pipe cleaners in different colors
✔ Scissors
✔ Googly eyes
✔ Glue
✔ Marker

LADYBUG

Wind a red short spiral. Make a black ball. Cut a short piece of black pipe cleaner, bend it in half, and wrap it around the head. For the antennae, bend the ends so they stick out. Push the ball into the spiral. Make dots on the body with a marker. Glue on googly eyes.

Spiral

Add black V shape

Make dots

INCHWORM

Cut five pipe cleaners in half. Use a pencil to make spirals. Bend a purple pipe cleaner in half to make the body. Twist the two ends together. Cut a small piece of yellow pipe cleaner. Bend it into a V shape for **antennae**. Attach the V to the purple pipe cleaner. Slide the colorful spirals onto the body. Glue googly eyes to the face.

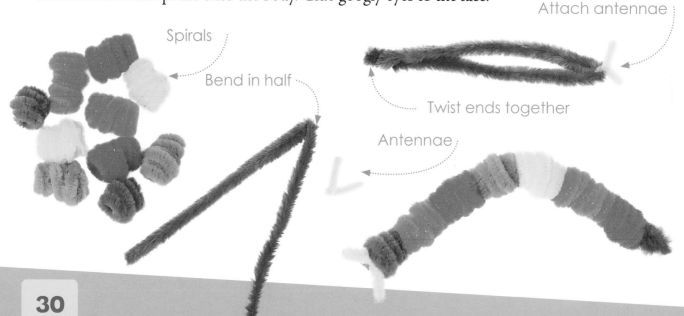

Spirals

Bend in half

Attach antennae

Twist ends together

Antennae

SPIDER

1 For the spider's body, make a ball out of a giant blue pipe cleaner. Cut a 2-inch (5 cm) piece of brown pipe cleaner. Wrap it around the body. Leave the ends sticking out.

Twist

Spread out

2 Cut two more brown pipe cleaners in half. Line up the four pieces. Wrap another brown pipe cleaner around the middle. Fan the legs out and bend them in half.

Bend

3 Attach the body to the legs using the brown pipe cleaner from Step 1. Glue googly eyes onto the spider's face.

GLOSSARY

antennae Long body parts used to sense things found on the heads of most insects.

chenille A soft, fuzzy material.

petals Soft, colorful parts of a flower that are often brightly colored.

spokes Bars that connect the inside of a wheel to the outside.

FOR MORE INFORMATION

Further Reading

Boutique-Sha. *Making Pipe Cleaner Pets.*
East Petersburg, PA: Fox Chapel Publishing, 2013.

Clair, Alice. *Fat Fuzzies.*
Richmond, BC: SpiceBox Books, 2013.

Petelinsek, Kathleen. *Creating Pipe Cleaner Crafts.*
North Mankato, MN: Cherry Lake Publishing, 2014.

WEBSITES

For web resources related to the subject of this book, go to: www.windmillbooks.com/weblinks and select this book's title.

INDEX